ACKNOWLEDGMENTS

The editor and publisher have made every effort to trace the owner-ship of all copyrighted material and to secure permission from copyright holders of such material. In event of any question arising to the use of any material, the publisher and editor, while expressing regret for inadvertent error, will be pleased to make any necessary corrections in future printings.

Quote from THE ART SPIRIT by Robert Henri. Copyright © 1923 by J.B. Lippincott Company. Copyright renewed 1951 by Violet Organ. Reprinted by permission of HarperCollins Publishers Inc.

Reprinted by permission of the publishers and the Trustees of Amherst College from THE POETS OF EMILY DICKINSON, Thomas H. Johnson, ed., Cambridge, Mass.: The Belknap Press of Harvard University Press, Copyright © 1951, 1955, 1979, 1983 by the President and Fellows of Harvard College.

Excerpts by William James reprinted by permission from Harvard University Press, Cambridge, Mass. Copyright © Harvard University Press. All rights reserved.

Quote from AT THE BACK OF THE NORTH WIND by George MacDonald Copyright © Penguin USA, New York, NY. All rights reserved.

Quote from A BACKWARD GLANCE by George Jean Natham Copyright © Alfred A Knopf, Inc., New York, NY 10022. All rights reserved.

Quote from THE ENJOYMENT OF LAUGHTER by Max Eastman Copyright © Simon & Schuster, New York, NY 10020. All rights reserved.

Excerpt from TENDENCIES IN MODERN AMERICAN POETRY by Amy Lowell. Copyright, 1921, by Houghton Mifflin Company. Reprinted by permission of Houghton Mifflin Co. All rights reserved.

Published by The C.R. Gibson Company, Norwalk, Connecticut 06856
ISBN 0-8378-6948-X
GB528

Lifelines

A Treasure Chest of Words to Conquer the Stormy Seas

Robert B. Luce

Illustrated by George Shedd

The C.R. Gibson Company • Norwalk, Connecticut • 06856

Introduction

Sailors know about lifelines. There is always one coiled and handy on the stern of any vessel, ready to be tossed to a passenger or crew member who has gone overboard. If you have ever needed a lifeline, you know how welcome it is, how it feels to be hauled back on board to the waiting arms of a friend or rescuer.

On shore we are often in need of lifelines, too, whether we are swimming in a calm sea in little danger, or drowning in a stormy sea in the darkness.

Words can be lifelines, as welcome and reassuring as a coil of rope. This book is a collection of written lifelines for you to grasp when you need solace, inspiration, when you are in sorrow or grief, or fearful of the future.

We all have periods of anxiety. You are not alone in yours. We lose our zest for life and for nature. We forget the blessings we do have. We feel the need for love, companionship, we lose hope for tomorrow.

The lifelines in this book were written, some of them, centuries ago—some of them only recently. Old or new, they are here to provide you with rescue from your own sea of troubles.

Robert B. Luce

Inspiration for Today and Tomorrow

Do you ever wonder how it is that certain of your friends or family members are inspired to overcome odds, or to take an unexpected step that gets them out of a rut?

Or, on a wider scale, man's history brims with examples of achievements and victories, large and small, that have been recorded by men and women who have found it within themselves to persevere when life seemed empty, or worse, hopeless.

"Being stuck" is by no means a unique experience. It happens, and the longer it lasts the more difficult it is to get going again.

The inspiration to break out may come from any source: a poem, a conversation with a friend, a walk in the woods—

anything that leads us to take even a small step toward a break-out, a change in our patterns, can be a lifeline.

If these words prompt you to make one small move in a new direction, they will have earned their place here.

R.L.

Perseverance is a great element of success. If you only knock long enough, you are sure to wake up somebody.

Henry Wadsworth Longfellow

If man does not keep pace with his companions, perhaps it is because he hears a different drummer. Let him step to the music which he hears, however measured or far away.

Henry David Thoreau

I seem to have been only like a boy playing on the seashore, diverting myself now and then finding a pebble or a prettier shell than ordinary, whilst the great ocean of truth lay all undiscovered about me.

Isaac Newton

I have believed in love and work, and their linkage. I have believed that we are neither angels nor devils, but humans, with clusters of potentials in both directions. I am neither an optimist or a pessimist, but a possibilist.

Max Lerner

Lost: Somewhere between sunrise and sunset, two golden hours, each set with sixty diamond minutes. No reward is offered, for they are gone forever.

Horace Mann

Make use of your life while you have it. Whether you have lived enough depends on yourself, not on your number of years.

Michael de Montaigne

Do not shorten the morning by getting up late. Look upon it as the quintessence of life.

Arthur Schopenhauer

Look not mournful into the past. It comes not back again. Wisely improve the Present. It is thine. Go forth to meet the shadow future, without fear and with a manly heart.

Henry Wadsworth Longfellow

*I am only one
But still I am one.
I cannot do everything,
But I can do something.
And because I cannot do everything
I will not refuse to do the one thing that
I can do.*

Edward Everett Hale

*We never know how high we are
Until we are called to rise
And then, if we are true to plan
Our statures touch the skies!*

Emily Dickinson

Go confidently in the direction of your dreams. Live the life you have imagined. As you simplify your life, the laws of the universe will be simpler, solitude will not be solitude, poverty will not be poverty, nor weakness, weakness.

Henry David Thoreau

Facing Fears...

Real and Imagined

Fears come in two varieties — those that are prudent — the fear of violence, or the fear of natural disasters, or of injury or death in an automobile accident.

The other fears are within us, and they are legion. We fear failure. We fear criticism. We fear the future. We fear illness. More seriously, there are phobias, fear of flying, fear of strangers, fear of venturing out.

It is these inner fears that are the most universal and the most prevalent throughout history. Conquering these fears is a matter of stripping away the ghosts and goblins and the paranoias that nurture fear within us.

Where then do we find the inner strength and courage to combat these inner fears? To shrink them into their true proportions and see them for what they are?

To start, take this bit of wisdom from Lucretius who lived 2,000 years ago: *For as children tremble and fear everything in the blind darkness, so we in the light sometimes fear what is no more to be feared than the things children in the dark hold in terror and imagine will come true.*

R.L.

Nothing in life is to be feared, it is only to be understood.

Marie Curie

Our doubts are traitor,
And make us lose the good we oft might win
By fearing to attempt.

William Shakespeare

The only courage that matters is the kind that gets you from
one moment to the next.

Mignon McLaughlin

Not in the clamor of the crowded street,
Nor in the shouts and plaudits of the throng,
But in ourselves, are triumph and defeat.

Henry Wadsworth Longfellow

Courage is resistance to fear, mastery of fear—not absence of fear.

Mark Twain

He who fears he will suffer, already suffers from his fear.

Michael D. Montaigne

You gain strength, courage and confidence by every experience in which you really stop to look fear in the face. You must do the thing which you think you cannot do.

Eleanor Roosevelt

It is only by risking our persons from hour to hour that we live at all. And often our faith beforehand in an uncertified result is the only thing that makes the result come true...Be not afraid of life. Believe that life is worth living, and your belief will help create the fact.

William James

Heroism, the Caucasian mountaineers say, is endurance for one moment more.

George Kennan

You don't learn to hold your own in the world by standing guard, but by attacking and getting well hammered yourself.

George Bernard Shaw

Fear is the main source of superstition, and one of the main sources of cruelty. To conquer fear is the beginning of wisdom.

Bertrand Russell

The first and greatest commandment is: Don't let them scare you.

Elmer Davis

Give me the spirit that on life's rough sea
Loves t'have his sails fill'd with a lusty wind,
Even till his sail-yards tremble, his masts crack,
And his rapt ship run on her side so low
That she drinks water, and her keel ploughs air;
There is no danger to a man, that knows
What life and death is; there is not any law
That exceeds his knowledge; neither is it lawful
That he should stoop to any other law.
He goes before them, and commands them all...

George Chapman

A ship in harbor is safe, but that is not what ships are built for.

John A. Shedd

Losses...

A Survival Guide

To go through the stages of life is to suffer losses. We pass from birth to youth to old age and eventual death. We also have gains and triumphs along the way. When the losses occur, we often forget those moments past—we are so over-whelmed by the present.

The losses that are the result of the inevitable biological clock ticking are not easy to bear, but they are predictable...the loss of youthful vigor, the greying of the hair, the gradual slow-ing down.

It is the losses that result from unexpected events, circum-stances over which we have no control that cause the acute pain and suffering...the loss of a spouse, a child, or a dear friend, the loss of a home place, the feeling of not having the value you once had in society, the loss of love or work, or wonder.

Some losses are momentary, some ineradicable; some

minor, some monumental and inconsolable. Here perhaps, you will find consolation.

First, to gain some perspective, consider this, which is as true today as it was in the moment it was written by Socrates: *If all the misfortunes of mankind were cast into a basket, in order to be equally distributed among all, those who now think themselves to be unhappy would much prefer the share they already possess to that which would fall to them by such a division.*

R.L.

Why destroy your present happiness by a distant misery which may never happen at all?—for every substantial grief has twenty shadows, and most of the shadows are of your own making.

Sydney Smith

The way to mourn the dead is to take care of the living who belong to them.

Edmund Burke

The tomb is not a blind alley, it is a thoroughfare. It closes on the twilight, it opens on the dawn.

Victor Hugo

It is dangerous to abandon one's self to the luxury of grief; it deprives one of courage, and even of the wish for recovery.

Henry Ameil

*Man was made for joy and woe
And when this we rightly know,
Safely through the world we go.*

William Blake

Sorrows are like thunderclouds. Far off they look black, but directly over us merely grey.

Jean Paul Richter

This is my last message to you: In sorrow seek happiness.

Fyodor Dostoyevsky

*Out of the night that covers me,
Black as the pit from pole to pole
I thank whatever Gods may be
For my unconquerable soul.*

W. E. Henley

I don't know why it is we are in such a hurry to get up
when we fall down. You might think we would lie there and
rest a while.

Max Eastman

Why, why repine, my pensive friend,
At pleasures slipped away?
Some the stern fates will never lend,
And all refuse to stay.

I see the rainbow in the sky,
The dew upon the grass;
I see them, and I ask not why
They glimmer as they pass.

With folded arms I linger not
To call them back; t'were in vain:
In this, or some other spot
I know they'll shine again.

Walter Savage Landor

The rich spoils of memory are mine, Mine too, are the
precious things of today—books, flowers, pictures, nature
and sports...The best of life is always further on...Age is not
all decay; it is the ripening—the swelling for fresh life
within, that withers and bursts the husk.

George MacDonald

Remember me when I am gone away
Gone far away into the silent land;
Yet if you should forget me for a while
And afterward remember, to not grieve;
For if the darkness and corruption leave
A vestige of the thought I once had.
Better by far you should forget and smile
Than you should remember and be sad.

Christina Rossetti

Reaching Out...

Sharing Life with Others

There are those who seek the joys of solitude...times when peace and meditation can be a lifeline. But there is a vast gulf between solitude and loneliness. Loneliness, seldom if ever, is a choice.

In a nutshell, solitude "is a good place to visit, but a poor place to stay," according to Josh Billings, our American humorist.

In our time, loneliness has become a familiar companion for those who have few or no family members nearby, for single people, for young or old, rich or poor. No one is immune. Even those who seem untouched—married people, for example—may find themselves lonely in their marriage.

Of all the maladies that might befall you the good news is that it is curable. Reaching out is not always easy, but you soon discover that by reaching out you may be helping the person you reach out to as much as you are helping yourself.

When the subject is solitude, Emily Dickinson, the poet "maid of Amherst" comes to mind.

She lived a life of solitude, self-chosen. Most of her delicate, elegant poetry is about other matters, but all of her poems stem from her solitary viewpoint, and many of them have solitude as a theme.

Her passionate messages from her world to ours were her

way of reaching out, messages of lasting beauty that will never fade...

If I can stop one heart from breaking,
I shall not live in vain.
If I can ease one life the aching,
Or cool one pain,
Or help one fainting robin
Unto his nest again,
I shall not live in vain.

R.L.

The happiness of life is made up of minute fractions—the little soon forgotten charities of a kiss or a smile, a kind look, a heartfelt compliment.

Samuel Taylor Coleridge

I shall not pass through this world but once; any good thing therefore that I can do, or any kindness that I can show to my fellow creature, let me do it now, let me not defer nor neglect it. I may not pass this way again.

Ettienne de Grille

Friendship, compounded of esteem and love, derives from one its tenderness and its permanence from the other.

Samuel Johnson

O! many a shaft at random sent
Finds mark the archer never meant!
And many a word, at random spoken,
May soothe or wound a heart that's broken!

Sir Walter Scott

Unless we think of others and do something for them, we miss one of the great sources of happiness.

Ray Lyman Wilbur

In this world you need to be a bit too kind in order to be kind enough.

Pierre Carlet De Chamberlain de Marivaux

Without friends, the world is but a wilderness...
There is no man that imparteth his joys to his friends but he joyeth more; and no man that imparteth his griefs to a friend, but he grieveth the less.

Francis Bacon

There is much satisfaction in work well done,
praise is sweet; but there can be no happiness
equal to the joy of finding a heart that understands.

Victor Robinson

Who is more indefatigable in toil, when there is occasion for
toil, than a friend? Who is readier to rejoice in one's good
fortune? Whose praise is sweeter? From whose lips does
one learn the truth with less pain? What fortress, what
bulwarks, what arms are more steadfast than loyal hearts?

Saint John Chrysostom

To love thy neighbor as ourself is such a fundamental truth
for regulating human society, that by that alone one might
determine all the cases in social morality.

John Locke

The more we know, the better we forgive;
Whoever feels deeply, feels for all who live.

Madame de Stael

...And hold of dearest worth:
Light of the sapphire skies,
Peace of the silent hills,
Shelter of the forests, comfort of the grass,
Shadows of the clouds that swiftly pass,
And after the showers,
The smell of flowers
And of the good brown earth—
And best of all, along the way, friendship and mirth.

Henry Van Dyke

Rest For Our Soul...

Nature's Gift

We have been endowed with a priceless gift—the natural world. From our beginnings, balm for a troubled soul has been there for us in nature's endless and infinite wonders.

The tiny planet we live in—its plains, mountains, seas, clouds, stars, forests and quiet lakes, vast deserts, have inspired and awed us through recorded time.

It is a part of us, that natural world, and when we get too far out of touch with it, we lack nourishment, and if we can, we try to return to what we have lost along the way. For some it is the peace of a quiet stream, for others it is to do battle with a storm on the high seas, or to sample the delight of a field of wildflowers.

And when we visit nature, more often than not, we find more than we sought—a realization that there is a need to be grateful, and to stand in awe.

Down through the centuries, the peoples of the earth have created ceremonies and religions to worship the unknown architect of our natural world.

As you will see, nature is a lifeline for the soul—for the deepest part of us, for we are all children of nature.

R.L.

My heart leaps up when I behold
A rainbow in the sky;
So it was when my life began
So it is now when I am a man;
So be it when I grow old,
Or let me die!

William Wordsworth

Heaven to me's a fair blue stretch of sky,
Earth's just a dusty road.

John Masefield

Oh you poor folk in the cities,
Heaping the fairy gold that withers and died;
One field in June weather
Is worth all the gold ye gather,
One field in June weather—Paradise.

Katherine Tynan

The man who has seen the rising moon break out of the
clouds at midnight has been present like an archangel at
the creation of light and the world.

Ralph Waldo Emerson

The soft south wind, the flowers amid the grass,
The fragrant earth, the sweet sounds everywhere,
Seemed gifts too great almost for man to bear.

William Morris

I believe a leaf of grass is no less
than the journey work of the stars'
And the pimsire is equally perfect, and a grain of sand and
the egg of the wren
And the tree-toad is a chef d'oeuvre for the highest,
And the running blackberry would adorn
the parlors of heaven,
And the narrowest hinge in my hand puts to scorn
all machinery,
And the cow crunching with depressed head
surpasses any statue,
And a mouse is miracle enough
to stagger sextillions of infidels.

Walt Whitman

The impulse from a vernal wood
May teach you more of man,
Of moral evil and good
Than all the sages can.

William Wordsworth

What I call God. And fools call Nature.

Robert Browning

Summer afternoon—summer afternoon—to me those have always been the two most beautiful words in the English language.

Edith Wharton

Dawn is the fountainhead of light, hope and love, at dawn Nature awakens and all creatures, roused from sleep and strengthened, assemble anew...At dawn I look upon Nature and a fresh vitality seems to be filling mountains, hills, woods, and fields, I observe various and manifold beauties, and my mind is at ease when I mark and see them. When I perceive and note these miracles I am filled with the spirit that created them.

Ljudevit Vulicevic

So let the way be up the hill or down,
O'er rough or smooth, the journey will be joy,
Still seeking what I sought when but a boy.

Henry Van Dyke

There is a pleasure in the pathless woods,
There is rapture on the lonely shore,
There is society where none intrudes.
By the deep Sea, and music in its roar
I love not man the less, but Nature more.
From these our interviews, in which I steal
From all I may be, or have been before,
To mingle with the Universe, and feel
What I can ne'er express, yet cannot all conceal.

Lord Byron

To him who in the love of nature holds
Communion with her visible forms, she speaks
A various language; for his gayer hours
She has a voice of gladness, and a smile
And eloquence of beauty, and she glides
Into his darker musings, with a mild
And healing sympathy, that steals away
Their sharpness, ere he is aware.

William Cullen Bryant

Nature never did betray the heart that loved her.

William Wordsworth

The Human Spirit...

A Precious Legacy

We turn from nature to the wealth of the human spirit, another gift, just as awesome, but of a different stamp. Nature is eternal—the human spirit is eternally changing, striving—and enduring.

In the works of the spirit, we can find inspiration for our most jaded moments, affirmation of man's ability to soar to the heights of creativity—in poetry, music, art, architecture, dance, song, and story.

The creation can be as humble as a tidy verdant farm, a

small village on a mountain top, or as majestic as a magnificent bridge, a schooner or an ocean liner—each is testimony to human achievement, and to our striving for the best that is in us.

This heritage is there for us to take into our own spirit—to remind us that there is joy and hope, and that we can share in the joy that others have provided.

R.L.

Art comes to you proposing frankly to give nothing but the highest quality to your moments as they pass.

Walter Pater

Art is the desire of man to express himself, to record the reactions of his personality to the world he lives in.

Amy Lowell

Every man who has shown the way to beauty, to true culture, has been a rebel...who has found his people everywhere, a man whom all the world recognizes, accepts, whether he speaks through music, words or form.

Robert Henri

There is no music in Nature, neither melody nor harmony. Music is the creation of man.

H.R. Hawes

Music is the universal language of mankind—poetry their universal pastime and delight.

Henry Wadsworth Longfellow

The man that hath no music in himself,
Nor is not moved by the concord of sweet sounds,
Is fit for treason, stratagems and spoils.

William Shakespeare

Music is the medicine of the mind.

Walter Haddon

Music's the cordial of a troubled breast,
The softest remedy that grief can find;
The gentle spell that charms our care to rest
And calms the ruffled passions of the mind.
Music does all our joys refine,
And gives relish to our wine.

John Oldham

Men, even when alone, lighten their labors by song,
however rude.

Quintillian

I care not who write the laws of a country, so long as I may
listen to its songs.

George Jean Nathan

Only to Beauty Time belongs;
Men may perish, but not their songs.

Louis Ginsburg

I learnt life from the poets.

Madame de Stael

Poetry is simply the most beautiful, impressive and widely effective mode of saying things, and hence its importance.

Matthew Arnold

*I wish our clever young poets would remember my homely definitions of prose and poetry; that is, prose = words in their best order; poetry = the **best** words in the best order.*

Samuel Coleridge

It is not enough for poems to have beauty; they must have charm, and lead the hearer's soul where they will.

Horace

If a writer has to rob his mother, he will not hesitate; "Ode to a Grecian Urn" is worth any number of old ladies.

William Faulkner

Doth it not thrill thee Poet,
Dead and dust though thou art,
To feel how I press thy singing
Close to my heart?

Richard Le Gallienne

Ah to build, to build, to build
That is the noblest of all the arts.
Painting and sculpture are but the images,
Are merely shadows cast by outward things.
On stone and canvas, having in themselves
No separate existence. Architecture,
Existing in itself, and in seeming
A something it is not, surpasses them
As substance shadow.

Henry Wadsworth Longfellow

The ultimate justification of a work of art is to make the
spectator become a work of art himself.

Bernard Berenson

The artist appeals to the part of our being which is not
dependent on wisdom...and therefore more enduring. He
speaks to our capacity for delight and wonder, to the sense
of mystery surrounding our lives, our sense of pity and
beauty and pain.

Joseph Conrad

Art is man's refuge from adversity.

Menander

The subject matter of art is life,
life as it actually is;
but the function of art is to
make life better.

George Santayana

Finding Your Faith

Since recorded history mankind has sought the meaning of life, has worshipped at a thousand altars, and to as many gods, has endured life on earth for the promise of rewards in death, has believed in the immortality of the soul.

The deeper his suffering, the greater the need to believe in a God who cares, who can be prayed to, who will provide solace in the present moment, rewards in heaven, eternal life after death.

The common element is faith. It has sustained men and women in war, in slavery and bondage, victims of the holocaust, political prisoners and countless souls throughout history. Faith will not fail you when seeking solace.

Nowhere is faith more clearly voiced than by the Psalmists 61:3-6: *Hear my cry, O God, attend unto my prayer From the end of the earth I will cry unto thee, when my heart is overwhelmed, lead me to a rock that is higher than I. For thou has been a shelter for me, and a strong tower from the enemy. I will abide in thy tabernacle forever; I will trust in the cover of thy wings. For thou, O God, hast heard my vows; thou hast given me the heritage of those that fear thy name.*

R.L.

All who call on God, in true faith, earnestly from the heart, shall be heard, will receive what they asked and have desired.

Martin Luther

No coward soul is mine
No trembler in the world's storm-troubled sphere;
I see glories shine,
And faith shines equal, arming me from fear.

Emily Bronte

Reason is our soul's left hand,
Faith her right,
By these we reach divinity.

John Donne

The sovereign cure for worry is prayer.

William James

I am always content with what happens, for I think what
God chooses is better than what I choose.

Epiticus

More things are wrought by prayer than this world
dreams of.

Alfred Lord Tennyson

A bending staff I would not break,
A feeble faith I would not shake,
Not even rashly pluck away
The error which some truth may stay
Whose loss might leave the soul without
A shield against the shafts of doubt.

John Greenleaf Whittier

Have courage for the great sorrows of life and patience for
the small ones; when you have laboriously accomplished
your daily tasks, go to sleep in peace, God is awake.

Victor Hugo

Let nothing disturb thee,
Nothing affright thee
God never changeth;
Patient endurance
Attaineth all things.
Who God posesseth
In nothing is wanting;
Alone God sufficeth.

Saint Theresa

Cause us, O Lord our God, to lie down each night in peace, and to awaken each morning to renewed life and strength. Spread over us the tabernacle of Thy peace. Help us to order our lives by Thy counsel, and lead us into the paths of righteousness. Be Thou a shield about us, protecting us from hate and war, from pestilence and sorrow. Curb Thou also within us the inclination to do evil, and shelter us beneath the shadow of Thy wings. Guard our going out and our coming into life unto life and peace from this time forth and for evermore.

Services for the New Year—Yom Kippur

All fear is a sign of want of faith.

Ghandi

I cannot conceive how a man can look up into the heavens and say there is no God.

Abraham Lincoln

When I would beget content, and increase confidence in the power and wisdom and providence of the Almighty God, I will walk in the meadows of some gliding stream, and there contemplate the lilies that take no care, and those very many other little living creatures that are not only created but fed (a man knows not how) by the goodness of the God of Nature, and therefore trust in him.

Isaak Walton

I never saw a moor,
I never saw the sea;
Yet I know how the heather looks,
and what a wave may be.
I never spoke with God
nor visited in heaven,
yet certain I am of the spot
As if the chart were given.

Emily Dickinson

Epilogue

For whatever reason you happen to be holding this book in your hand, I pray that you have found something of value here. Some inspiration, some new thoughts, some perspective on the variety of human experience—and the richness and wonder of our being here on this small planet.

You will not, I hope, keep this book to yourself, but share your favorite portions with others who may also be needing your concern, and some cheer, solace, or courage.

In choosing the poems, passages, and short observations, I have looked for diversity, for wisdom from every age, and from some little known, even anonymous authors, as well as from those whose thoughts and observations will be with us for generations to come.

Looking back on my own life experiences, I can assure you that I know no one whose life has not been touched in some way by loneliness, self-doubt, losses, and frustrations.

Often I have been called upon to console family or friends at difficult times, and have received the same kindness from others in my own moments of need. So when working on this collection, I sought for words to pass on that were meaningful in a very personal sense.

For example, I love the sea and sailing, and nature in all of its guises, and I'm sure that my reverence shows.

My life has been spent in communion with art and music and that, too, is evident.

My own faith, I confess, is in our mysterious ability to endure against odds, and at the same time to create beauty, to keep our eyes set on the future.

In this small volume are words that have enriched me, and perhaps, through me, will enrich the lives of my children and grandchildren.

Robert B. Luce

Designed by Bob Pantelone
Edited by Julie Mitchell
Type set in Korinna
Printed on Warren Patina Matte